Friends and flowers give pleasure just by being.

FOR

FROM

Visit us on the Web at www.Hallmark.com.

ISBN: 1-59530-114-3

Designed by Koechel Peterson & Associates, Minneapolis, MN

Printed and bound in China

BOK4135

Friendship in Bloom

GIFT BOOKS
from Hallmark

As we journey through life,

we find special friends,

each as lovely as a flower

blossoming with a beauty

all its own.

AND, FRIENDS, LIKE FLOWERS,

are more beautiful

when they're together.

LIKE TWO DIFFERENT FLOWERS

growing in the same garden,

good friends share whatever sunshine

or showers may come their way.

The happiness, tears, and love

they share are the soil,

water, and sunshine

that nurture the brightest blossoms.

THEY NEED EACH OTHER TO BLOOM.

Friends are the flowers in our meadows,

the sunshine in our skies.

When two share the same path,

the way is not straighter

or the sun brighter.

They only seem that way.

And the path friends travel together

blossoms with happy moments

AS BEAUTIFUL AS ALL THE FLOWERS OF SUMMER.

WITHIN THE GARDEN OF FRIENDSHIP,

each flower grows

in its own special way....

nurtured by kindness and caring,

roots grow deep and strong...

and petals unfold with beautiful moments

to keep forever in your heart.

GOOD FRIENDS SHARE A GARDEN OF MEMORIES.

SUN-BRIGHT AND SOFT PASTEL,

EACH COLOR

ADDS ITS BEAUTY

TO THAT LOVELY LANDSCAPE.

A single rose may be your garden...

a single friend, your world.

LIKE WILDFLOWERS,

friends may be different,

yet bloom beautifully together.

But, whether like a rose

or like a wildflower,

each friend has joy to share.

IN OUR LIFETIMES,

there are only so many perfect spring days…

only so many seasons of full bloom

with the sun overhead

and the air perfumed by flowers…

IN OUR LIFETIMES,

there are only so many genuine soul mates,

only a few who really know us

as we know them

and enjoy us for who we truly are.

Some friends shine in our lives

like a golden sun

in a winter sky.

They brighten our days

just as springtime

brings warmth and the promise of flowers

to the world after winter.

A special friend is like

an exquisite flower,

unique and lovely…

And a smile

from such a friend

is like the first blossom of spring.

Even when true friends

share the rain,

the outlook's always sunny.

JUST AS SUN AND RAIN

NURTURE EACH FLOWER,

friends encourage, comfort, and care.

A friend is a gifted gardener

who finds ways to help us bloom...

A seed or two of kindness,

a sprinkle of laughter…

before you know it,

friendship blossoms…

and you gather bouquets of happiness.

EVERY MOMENT IS A SEED

from which the flowers

of tomorrow's happiness

may grow.

Friends share a warm and sheltered space…

because a friend is that special person

with whom you always feel at home...

and her friendship is like a flower

that blooms with constant beauty.

THE COMFORT OF A FRIEND

is like a house wren's morning song…

like the fragrance of lilacs on the evening breeze…

It's like the splash of the garden brook,

or the sound of easy rain.

Sometimes flowers lean together

and touch their petals

like two friends exchanging

thoughts and secrets.

Friendship blooms like a poppy,

scattering seeds of joy in unexpected places.

THERE IS NO SUCH THING

as an ordinary flower—

no such thing as an ordinary friend.

IN THE GARDEN OF TRUE FRIENDSHIP,

the flowers bloom forever.

If you have enjoyed this book,
Hallmark would love to hear from you.

Please send comments to:

Book Feedback
2501 McGee, Mail Drop 215
Kansas City, MO 64141-6580

Or e-mail us at:

booknotes@hallmark.com